IMAGES OF WALES

THE
GRAND PAVILION

PORTHCAWL

IMAGES OF WALES

THE
GRAND PAVILION
PORTHCAWL

KEITH E. MORGAN

TEMPUS

*This book is dedicated to the late Cllr Russell Mabley JP,
founder of The Grand Pavilion, and to all those legions of
performers and patrons who have supported the facility
since its inception in 1932.*

Frontispiece: Welcome to the enchanting and bewitching world of
The Grand Pavilion. This imposing structure on the seafront at
Porthcawl has been a centre of attraction and a Mecca for
spellbinding entertainment for seventy-two years. The photograph
shows Helen Jeckells as 'Witch Hazel' in the 2003 Christmas
pantomime, *Beauty and the Beast.*

First published 2004

Tempus Publishing Limited
The Mill, Brimscombe Port,
Stroud, Gloucestershire, GL5 2QG
www.tempus-publishing.com

© Keith E. Morgan, 2004

British Library Cataloguing in Publication Data.
A catalogue record for this book is available from the British Library.

ISBN 0 7524 3256 7

Typesetting and origination by Tempus Publishing Limited.
Printed in Great Britain.

Contents

Foreword

I suppose I have had a love affair with Porthcawl and The Grand Pavilion for more than seventy years. Like all love affairs, there have been more than a few ups and downs along the way!

As a child I visited Porthcawl on numerous 'Whitsun Treat' outings from my home in Brynna, together with other members of the 'Band of Hope'. Later, as a young musician and performer, I played at The Pavilion in the latter stages of the war and made frequent return visits through the 1950s and '60s for one-off shows and charity appearances.

It was at the start of the 1970s that my involvement with The Pavilion became something of a crusade. The building was then run by the Porthcawl Council and was threatened with closure. I decided to mount South Wales' first ever summer show at the venue and *Summer Stars* was the result. It was a show designed to rival anything that other British holiday resorts could offer: comedy, singing, speciality acts and dancers, and a change of programme twice a week too for those who wanted more.

I put my own money into the project, called on performers who I knew and respected and took on the roles of presenter, producer, director, financier and even ticket seller, along with my wife Elizabeth and sons Roger and Ceri. A panto' followed that winter – *Billy and Bonzo meet Robin Hood*, and so began a decade of seasonal shows from my company. Not all of them featured myself, but I was fortunate enough to be able to call on fellow Welsh performers to present first-class family entertainment at a venue that soon became a firm favourite with seemingly everyone in South Wales, as well as visitors from all over the UK. It seemed as though every colliery, steel works and social club sent their children to our panto'.

Among those artistes who appeared along the way were vocalists Johnny Tudor, Bryn Williams, Peter Lewis, Lesley King, Julie DeMarco and Siân Hopkins, comedians Johnny Stewart, Ronnie Collis, Del Derrick, speciality acts such as The Falcons, Roy Lester and Paula Lee, Terry Hall and Lenny the Lion, Howell Evans and Patricia Kane, Bill Gore the Yodelling Cobbler, Shag Connors and the Carrot Crunchers and many more. Dancers included the fabulous Ballet Montmarte, and later a young lady who was to marry Paul Daniels – the lovely Debbie McGee! We even managed to have Currie's Dancing Waters in one of the summer seasons.

The Grand Pavilion was a lovely vibrant building to be involved with, due in no small part to the manager Ron Harris, who seemed to do all the jobs – even sweeping up! I also remember the loyal 'backstage crew' of electricians: Tom Rossam and Anthony Callaghan and stage manager Derek Harris –all local lads who loved The Pavilion dearly. The scenery was made and painted by a Polish wizard – Alan Mason, who also looked after the original 'real' Bonzo. Johnny Lister was my company manager for many seasons, with Gloria Williams and Lynn Mitchell in the box office. Margaret Wilkes was ever-present in the main office, with Roger Price directing operations back in the leisure department at Ogwr Borough (later Bridgend) Council. What a happy band we were!

My goodness, we had some great after-show parties, whether the business was good or bad! The fish and chips came from Sidoli's, there was always a great Sunday lunch at Jenny Fulgoni's, coffee at Alun Owens' 'Sospan Fach' and show photographs from his brother Kenneth Owens.

After a break of a few years, I returned to The Pavilion in 1986 with the panto' *Aladdin* and the response was as strong as I could have hoped for. By then, Martin Jenkins was manager, Cyril Warilow his assistant, Jane Saville was in the box office and Wayne Francis was electrician. So began another stay of six years for Christmas seasons. Performers included Olwen Rees, Ceri Dupree, Jenny Ogwen, Glyn Dawson, Johnny Dallas, Phil Howe and the marvellous Dot Watts Dancers and Babes, not forgetting outstanding musicians, Boyce and Ronnie Huxford. We were even responsible for bringing a baby into this world early, as his mum went into premature labour through laughing so much during a performance of *Mother Goose*!

It has now been more than twelve years since I performed at The Pavilion, yet people still ask me if I am in Porthcawl for panto'! It is funny how you can work all over Britain and the world, and yet become synonymous with one place. I hope it might still be possible to see *Billy & Bonzo* at The Pavilion once more before I hang up my clown boots.

I do hope you enjoy this book and the memories it will evoke. Certainly while hunting out some of my old photographs and posters, it sent my mind back over some very happy times.

Stan Stennett, MBE, FRWCMD

Preface

It gives me great pleasure to introduce this collection of photographs of The Grand Pavilion, Porthcawl. The Grand Pavilion is a venue that was built in 1932, just after the depression, with support from the local community. Originally intended as a dancehall, it is a building that has become the focal point of the community of the County Borough of Bridgend. We should treasure this venue that holds so many memories and which has given so much pleasure over the years. Buildings such as The Grand Pavilion are rare and, in my opinion, no modern building could replace its character and beauty.

My first experience, like many others, was a visit to see Stan Stennett in pantomime in the early '70s. I fell in love with the building then and still feel passionately about the venue today. The staff of The Grand Pavilion, both past and present, have all felt a deep commitment to the venue. Establishing the long-term future of The Grand Pavilion and providing quality entertainment to suit all patrons has always been our goal.

I hope you enjoy looking at all the images that portray the past and present, both on and off the boards. Life is a stage, and the stage is an important aspect of all our lives. The theatre is integral to improving the quality of our often stressful, modern way of life, giving us the opportunity to escape into the world of entertainment.

May I express my sincere gratitude to author Keith Morgan for compiling this book, and to those who also helped to provide valuable information to make this publication possible. Thank you also to Bridgend County Borough Council for giving me the opportunity to manage this fine old building and to Porthcawl Town Council for its support over the years.

Finally, my grateful thanks to all our patrons for supporting The Grand Pavilion in its struggle to survive in very turbulent times.

Jan Adkins, 2004

Jan Adkins – General Manager,
The Grand Pavilion (1998-2004).

Introduction and Acknowledgements

The Grand Pavilion is Porthcawl's 'Jewel-in-the-Crown'. When it was built and opened in 1932, modernity was considered to be the keynote of its architecture. The most significant feature was the large octagonal concrete dome directly surmounting the main auditorium and concert hall. A Grade II Listed building since 1998, the dome is a classic example of the early application of ferrous concrete (Ferrocrete) in building construction. Sited in a magnificent position on the seafront at Porthcawl, visitors to the town cannot fail to be impressed by the character of the white painted Grand Pavilion. From its location on the Esplanade, The Grand Pavilion commands a broad and clear view across the wide expanse of the Bristol Channel, to both the English coastline and the western approaches of the Atlantic Ocean.

Over the years The Grand Pavilion has been a magnet for entertainment and has attracted a cavalcade of many well-known artistes and shows to its doors. In the days of the big bands, famous orchestras performed to a packed dance floor and many a budding romance developed into a long-term marriage. As well as being a focal point for parades and civic ceremonies, The Grand Pavilion is a venue for both amateurs and professionals alike. It has been home to concerts, recitals, operettas, ballet, boxing and wrestling contests, conferences, talent competitions, beauty contests, pantomimes, summer shows and the all-important Miners' Eisteddfod. The Grand Pavilion continues to be a centre of attraction and a venue for entertainment. Every encouragement is given to local choirs, schools and operatic societies, as well as to youth theatre and dance development groups, where workshops are set up to assist with learning. The management of The Grand Pavilion also operates a work experience programme with the local schools. Through this scheme, many youngsters put their first foot on the ladder to satisfy their ambitions in becoming theatrical performers.

In this book, I have strived to capture the rich history of The Grand Pavilion and to demonstrate its importance in helping to make and maintain Porthcawl as one of South Wales' major seaside resorts. It is an institution that is an integral part of our heritage. Generations have passed through the building's portals as both patrons and artistes. As such, we as a community have a bounden duty to do our utmost to ensure that The Grand Pavilion continues to be treasured and maintained for future generations to come.

I would not have been able to produce this book without assistance from a great many individuals and organisations. Foremost in my acknowledgements of the enthusiastic help that I have received, I would like to thank Jan Adkins – General Manager of The Grand Pavilion. In addition to writing the Preface, Jan and her team made me feel very welcome at The Grand Pavilion. They have given me freedom of access to any performance and have provided their unstinted support for all my needs in researching The Grand Pavilion's archives. I have tried to list all the team members individually below. Stan Stennett MBE comes next on my list: he has a wealth of information. As well as providing many of the photographs and records, he has also written a very fine Foreword to this book; one that I must say, I found very hard to follow with this Introduction. Dewi Roger Price, retired principal arts officer of Bridgend County Borough Council, together with Martin Jenkins, past General Manager of The Grand Pavilion, have also been of great help guiding me through the past records and activities of The Grand Pavilion.

As to organisations, I would like to record my thanks to the following for their co-operation: The South Wales Miners' Eisteddfod (secretary Dewi Roger Price); Brass Bands Competition, Contest Controller (the late Eifon W. Rogers); Porthcawl Town Council (Mayor Cllr Rosemary

Deere); Bridgend County Borough Council (Mayor Cllr Doug John); Porthcawl Amateur Operatic and Dramatic Society (president Dr David Parry, chairman Wyn Jones); Porthcawl Comprehensive School (Head Teacher K. Dykes); Porthcawl Civic Trust, (president David Cox); Paul Holman Associates (Christmas Pantomimes) Director Paul Holman (associate director Adrian Jeckells); The Porthcawl Male Choir (president Glan Davies, chairman Owain Jones); Porthcawl Museum & Historical Society (chairman John David, secretary Gwyn Petty); The RAFA Club (secretary Glen Evans); Porthcawl Townswomen's Guild (secretary Beryl Jones); Gloria Hill Academy of Dance (proprietor Gloria Hill); Bridgend County Borough Council Library Services (John Wood, county librarian and staff), Porthcawl Branch Library, Leslie Milne, (librarian and staff).

The response I have received from individuals and performers has been fantastic. My grateful thanks are due to: Peter Alexander, Graham Anderson, Pat and Wyndham Angell, Raul Arrieta, John Blundell, Cllr Megan Butcher, Anthony Callaghan, Julie Cane, Helena Colclough, Christopher Colquhoun, Linda Coombes, David Cox, Brian Davies, Steve Dennis, Mary Ellen Devery, Wayne Francis, John Fry (freelance photography), Sheila Gammon, Carol and Phillip George, Margaret Griffiths, Claire Harding, Nigel Harding, Derek Harris, Norman Harris, the late Ron Harris, Rosie Hartnell (Valley Music Ltd), Mair Harrhy, Derek Harris, Anne and Clive Hayward, Bert (the late) and Glenys Hayward, Andrew Hillier, Breda (Brenda) Hole, Andrea and Nigel Hopkins, Jacqueline Hopkins, Michelle Hopkins, Pauline Hopkins, Gary Iles, Vivien Inglis, Florence E. James, Joan Jones, Patricia Jones, Matthew Knight, Aubrey Lewis, Nigel Lewis-Davidson, Ron P. Lewis, Andrew Lougher-Harris, Jan and Roger Lynall, Patricia Mabley, Michael J. Mansley, Cllr Madeleine and Steve Moon, Craig Martin, Malcolm F. Nugent, Pollyanna Orr (Clive Conway Celebrity Productions Ltd), Tyrone O'Sullivan OBE, Doreen and Benjamin Owen, Keith Owen (always and forever), Hywel Owens, the late Kenneth Owens (photographer), Katy Pask, Mark Phillips, Heather Protheroe, Joyce Lorena Raymond, Norma and Mansel Rees, Marilyn Richards, Rob Rixon, the late Eifon W. Rogers, Rex Spooner, Ceinwen and David John Thomas, Georgia Thomas, the late Gordon R. Thomas (photographer), Rita Thomas, Romy Thomas, Andrew Wallen, Jennifer Wallen, Joyce and Brian Webb, Evelyn and Vernon White, Patricia (née O'Neill) and Patrick Wheatley, Claire Williams, John Williams, Serena Williams, and all those amateur artistes that I photographed whilst they were appearing in The Grand Pavilion.

I would also like to express my thanks to the following professional artistes who were so patient and co-operative when they were having their photographs taken, especially as in some instances, this was during their on-stage performance: Lauren Adams, Beverley Sisters, Shân Cothi, Paul Daniels, Wayne Dobson, Richard Grieve, Keith 'appy Hopkins, Helen Jeckells, Peter Karrie, Debbie McGee, Joe Pasquale, Andrew Piper, Siân Phillips, Ian Smith, and Iris Williams OBE.

My penultimate acknowledgement has to be to Tempus Publishing Limited, for agreeing to produce this book in the first place. Not a subject that they would normally have chosen to cover, they have, nevertheless, under the guidance of Publisher David Buxton and his team of Editors, Matilda Pearce, Rob Sharman, Darren Lusty and Nicola Sweet, pulled out all the stops to help me produce this book on The Grand Pavilion, Porthcawl, on time. Thank you all.

The above list seems endless. If I have missed out an acknowledgement, it is entirely unintentional and carries my unreserved apologies and general thanks to those in any way affected by my oversight.

Finally, I would like to thank my wife Malvina, for her patience and tolerance whilst I have been preparing this book, and for her support in proofreading the manuscript and checking the contents prior to publication.

Keith E. Morgan, Author

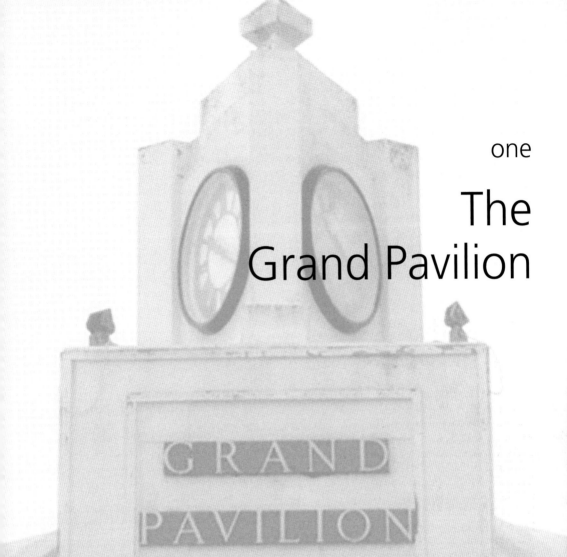

one

The
Grand Pavilion

A perspective view of the proposed Grand Pavilion, drawn by the architect E.J.E. Moore on 7 December 1931. The design was fabled to be based on a similarly styled building in Singapore!

The site for such a municipal building had been reserved, in their wisdom and foresight, by the Brogden family, the founders of Porthcawl. The Porthcawl Urban District Council had secured an option on this land in 1915, known as Brogden's Field, but the events of the First World War prevented any development at that time. Following the cutting of the first sod on 9 October 1931, the site was cleared and construction of the foundations for The Grand Pavilion began.

By early 1932, the structure of The Grand Pavilion was taking shape and construction had proceeded almost to the point where work could start on the erection of the ferrous concrete dome.

Preparing the construction of the octagonal dome for The Grand Pavilion. The picture, taken in 1932, shows George Matthews (arrowed), the carpenter and works engineer, with members of the building crew. Because of the importance of the use of ferrous concrete in the construction of the dome, The Grand Pavilion was given a Grade II listing in 1998.

The Grand Pavilion, Porthcawl, as it looked following completion in 1932. The picture serves to highlight the prestigious position the building occupies, facing the sea on the Esplanade. It was erected in record time. Estimated to cost £21,000 to build, the final figure for both The Grand Pavilion and Winter Gardens was £25,000.

Before officially opening The Grand Pavilion on 8 August 1932, Cllr Russell Mabley JP called upon Mrs J.H. Pearson, commandant of the Porthcawl detachment of the Red Cross, to unveil the two-faced clock, situated atop the front façade of the building. Supplied by H. Clare, jeweller of John Street, Porthcawl, and known as the Queen Alexandra Memorial Clock, it was erected by public subscription.

Cllr Russell Mabley JP, chairman of Porthcawl Urban District Council, together with Mrs Gladys Mabley, cutting the ribbon to perform the official opening ceremony of The Grand Pavilion on Monday 8 August 1932. The building of The Grand Pavilion was the brainchild of Cllr Mabley. Even though it had taken a lot to convince his fellow councillors, he was eventually been able to unite them in supporting a scheme to erect the edifice.

Cllr Russell Mabley JP and Mrs Gladys Mabley are seated at the centre with their son Vivian at their feet, surrounded by the many dignitaries who attended the opening ceremony of The Grand Pavilion.

Opening of	Grand Pavilion
ESPLANADE	PORTHCAWL
Monday, 8th	August, 1932
OFFICIAL	**BANQUET**
Esplanade Hotel,	*Porthcawl.*
RECEPTION at 6.30 p.m.	Ticket, 6/6
Name of Guest:	*Name of Guest:*
Table........ Seat No.	Table .... Seat No............

An inaugural dinner and dance was held on the evening of Monday 8 August 1932, to celebrate the opening of The Grand Pavilion.

More than 500 guests attended the official banquet that was held in the Esplanade Hotel, at which Cllr Russell Mabley JP presided. The Grand Pavilion was floodlit for the inaugural ball which followed; an event which was enjoyed by over 400 dancers.

THIS TABLET WAS UNVEILED BY

RUSSELL MABLEY ESQ. J.P
(CHAIRMAN OF THE PORTHCAWL URBAN DISTRICT COUNCIL)

ON 8TH AUGUST 1932

TO COMMEMORATE THE PUBLIC OPENING BY HIM OF THIS

PAVILION AND PALM COURT

THE COUNCIL
GRATEFULLY RECORD THE TOWN'S APPRECIATION
OF THE FINANCIAL ASSISTANCE RECEIVED FROM
HIS MAJESTYS GOVERNMENT

Above: One of the two bronze plaques unveiled by Cllr Russell Mabley JP, to commemorate the opening of The Grand Pavilion. The plaques are mounted either side of the exit doors at the rear of the auditorium.

Right: The gold plated key bearing the inscription 'Presented to Councillor Russell Mabley JP by Mr S.C. Taverner on the occasion of his opening The Pavilion, 8 August 1932.'

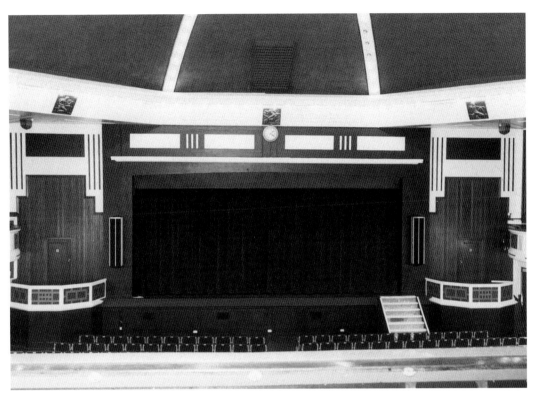

Above: The stage in the main auditorium. Note the original clock above the stage and the muses on the inner base rim of the octagonal dome. There are eight muses in all depicting 'Tragedy and Comedy', 'Astronomy', 'Art', 'Science', 'Religion', 'Poetry', 'Literature' and 'Music'.

Opposite above: The anchor mosaic on the top step which leads to the old main entrance of The Grand Pavilion. The anchor symbol formed the centrepiece of the Coat of Arms of the old Porthcawl Urban District Council. It reflected Porthcawl's dependence on the sea, once as an important port, and subsequently as a major holiday resort.

Opposite below: Inside the main entrance, showing the original box office and foyer of The Grand Pavilion.

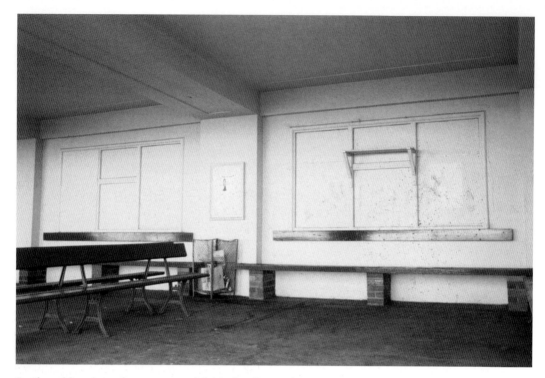

Porthcawl has always been renowned for its bracing qualities as it is close to the sea. To take advantage of this, The Grand Pavilion was designed to have open shelters on either side of the main entrance, where visitors could sit and enjoy the sea air in all weathers and in all seasons. Following the development of The Grand Pavilion in the early 1990s, the shelters were converted to administration offices and a café/bar.

This shows the original Winter Gardens in the grounds of The Grand Pavilion. They are now covered over with tarmac and relegated to use as a car park for the facility.

Bracing is not the word for it! The Grand Pavilion is under siege from rough seas. The Esplanade used to get a regular soaking during high tides, when the waves crashed over the promenade and flooded down into the town via John Street, Mary Street and Esplanade Avenue.

As quoted in the report on the opening of The Grand Pavilion in the 12 August 1932 issue of the *Glamorgan Gazette*, 'The sun shone out brilliantly all the while, and the quaint weather-vane set high above the pavilion – a galleon in bronze, with all sails set – glinted and glittered as if alive to the importance of this, its first voyage…' Its first voyage certainly lasted up to about 1972, after which time it was taken down from its prominent position, for some unknown reason, and stored away. In December 1996, it was resurrected. The picture shows Jason Crook, General Manager of The Grand Pavilion, holding the galleon weather-vane, prior to its remounting on the dome the following year in memory of H.E. and Peggy Dicks, the couple who ran and managed The Grand Pavilion during the Second World War.

Oops! The high tides and accompanying gales of January 1998 put paid to the galleon weather-vane. It was obviously too heavy a device for its mounting and was taken down in the interest of safety.

A new much lighter galleon weather-vane was purchased in 2003 by the Porthcawl Civic Trust Society. It was erected in commemoration of Her Majesty the Queen's Golden Jubilee of 3 June 2002. The first voyage of this new weather-vane was not plain sailing either; it also bent over in an ensuing storm and had to be re-erected with a stronger mounting.

two

Events

Top: Following its opening in 1932, The Grand Pavilion became the central location for most of the events that took place in Porthcawl from that time onwards. Carnivals were a speciality. This photograph from around 1936 shows Mary Callaghan née Davies being crowned as carnival queen with a young Derek Harris as her page boy. Derek's sister, Jean, is standing directly behind him.

Above: The Porthcawl Sea Cadets providing a Guard of Honour at The Grand Pavilion for the visit to the town by Mrs Winston Churchill, *c.* 1943. The Sea and Air Training Cadets were called upon to provide similar Guards of Honour for many important occasions.

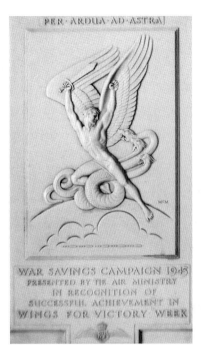

During the Second World War, The Grand Pavilion was used by many organisations as a meeting or assembly centre. It was also a rallying point for wartime collections, as the plaques (*above, left and right*) testify. The plaques are now on display in the Porthcawl Museum. Another event which centred on The Grand Pavilion was Battle of Britain Week. The photograph shows the 1956 Battle of Britain Queen with her attendants. It is not possible to identify anyone other than Joyce Lorena Mockett, who is seated first on the left.

Taking the salute outside The Grand Pavilion as the Army, Navy and Air Force marched past during Battle of Britain Week, 1956. The chairman of Porthcawl Urban District Council is accompanied on the dais by the Battle of Britain Queen and her attendants. Again, it is not possible to identify any of those in the photograph other than Joyce Lorena Mockett, who is on the immediate right of the saluting officer.

Cllr Mrs Madeleine Moon, Mayor of Porthcawl, in WAAF uniform, being driven past The Grand Pavilion in a US Army Willis Jeep during the 'We'll Meet Again' celebrations of 1992.

Many other events took place at The Grand Pavilion. Rita Thomas née O'Neil is hown (*above left*) being presented with a Cup after winning a talent competition during Battle of Britain Week in 1951. A young Carol George née Butler (*above right*) has just been presented with a St David's Day cycling proficiency test certificate on the stage of The Grand Pavilion by Cllr Cyril Phillips, chairman of Porthcawl Urban District Council, 1961.

The Grand Pavilion was always a good venue for foreign visitors. The photograph (*right*) shows a group of French students being welcomed to Porthcawl on 2 July 1973 by Cllr John David, chairman of Porthcawl Urban District Council.

Another favourite annual event held at The Grand Pavilion was the Beauty Queen competition. The winner of the Miss Porthcawl title in 1977 was twenty-one-year-old Shirley Williams of Pyle. The runner-up was sixteen-year-old Yvette Angell (left) of Kenfig Hill, while third place was taken by Karen Gregory, also of Kenfig Hill.

Ffynnon Dewi: Dewi's Well. An engraved stone presented by the National Association of Monumental Masons in 1962 , was accepted on behalf of the town by Cllr D. Neville Jones JP, chairman of the Porthcawl Urban District Council (bespectacled and wearing chain behind stone). After being displayed in The Grand Pavilion, the stone was erected alongside Dewi's Well in Nottage.

The Grand Pavilion was also a favourite venue for parties. This Christmas party given by the Distillers Company for children of employees of the Carbide Works at Kenfig, is in full swing. It was held in 1959 in the Lesser Hall (now the Victoria Rooms) in 1959. From left to right, front row: Frank Butler, Diane ?, Carol George née Butler, -?-.

Prime Minister John Major and Mrs Norma Major, captured on film outside The Grand Pavilion during the May 1996 Welsh Conservative Party Conference, by Graham Anderson. Security was intense for this visit. Drains were inspected and sealed days before the Prime Minister's arrival. On the big day, roads were cordoned off and armed police were mounted on The Grand Pavilion and adjoining buildings.

Porthcawl Townswomen's Guild has made great use of The Grand Pavilion since the branch was formed in January 1954. The picture shows a 'leisure and learning day', held by the Guild on 18 September 1999. The Guild Members are, from left to right: Beryl Davies, Joyce Webb, Edna Scone, Leslie Light and Glenis James.

A young Norman Harris with his father Ron in the grounds of The Grand Pavilion, July 1966. Ron Harris was a self-employed Commercial Artist who had his workshop underneath what are now the administration offices of The Grand Pavilion. The poster that is being held is typical of Ron's artwork. Ron went on to become manager of The Grand Pavilion from 1967 to 1974. With the skills inherited from his father, Norman started his succeddful business, 'Harris Printers of Porthcawl' in 1976.

three

Performers
and Artistes

The Grand Pavilion has been blessed with many clever and talented performers and artistes, both amateur and professional. Patricia Mabley (*left*) had the privilege of possibly being one of the first amateurs, if not one of the youngest, to perform at The Grand Pavilion. At the age of just five years and two months, she was awarded a Grade I certificate by the Royal Academy of Dancing, London, and invited to perform before Queen Mary at Cardiff. Patricia's first performance at The Grand Pavilion was at a pre-Second World War New Year's Eve party. Concealed inside an enormous snowball, she was pulled onto the ballroom floor on a sleigh. At the stroke of midnight, amid loud singing and illuminated by one huge spotlight, she popped out of the snowball in her ballet dress, holding a star. She continued dancing into her adolescence (*below right*) and during Dame Sybil Thorndike's (*below left*) tour through Wales in 1940, Patricia starred as one of the three witches in a performance of *Macbeth* on stage at The Grand Pavilion.

Sheila Gammon née Phillips (*above left and right*) was a contemporary of Patricia Mabley. She began her stage career at the tender age of four and entertained allied troops during the Second World War. Sheila produced her first show when she was sixteen and, by the time she had reached her nineteenth birthday, was running a regular annual children's show at The Grand Pavilion – *Porthcawl Steps Out*. Many local budding dance starlets started their stage careers with Sheila in these very popular shows. One of these was Marilyn Richards (*right*) who, as an adult, took part in RAFA shows and performances of the Porthcawl Amateur Operatic and Dramatic Society.

Left: Stepping Out at The Grand Pavilion, 1952. From left to right, top row: Marie Roberts, Lynn Morgan née Perkins, Ruth Davies née Rees. From left to right, bottom row: Sheila Richards, Vera Henderson née Hare, Barbara Powell née Seddon.

Below: The full assembly of the Sheila Phillips dance troupe, suitably attired for their performance of *There's a Little Dutch Mill on a Little Dutch Hill* for the July 1963 *Porthcawl Steps Out* show.

Right: Brynmor Williams, a long-standing friend of Patricia Mabley since childhood, went on to sing in the famous *Black and White Minstrel show,* as well as in Stan Stennett's summer shows and pantomimes.

Below: Another full assembly of the Porthcawl Steps Out girls in July 1963, this time posing in their ballet dresses on the steps leading down into the Winter Gardens.

Above: This captures two more well-known local amateur artistes acting in a 1950s panto' version of *Aladdin*. Howard Saunders (left) took the part of Widow Twankey, while Brian Webb played the wizard, Abernazer.

Left: The Porthcawl Amateur Operatic and Dramatic Society's production of *New Moon*. This ran in The Grand Pavilion from 9-14 April 1962. Gillian Woodcock who was around fourteen years of age, performed as a dancer, and Rob Rixon who was fifteen years old, as a Spaniard.

A scene from another Porthcawl Amateur Operatic and Dramatic Society's production, *Oklahoma*, in 1964. From left to right: Phillip George as Ike Skidmore, a very young Jeff John and Anthony Jones as Ali Hakim.

Evelyn White, another well-known local vocalist, first performed on stage at The Grand Pavilion at the age of eighteen as a soloist for the Afan Ladies Choir, Port Talbot. She has since appeared on several occasions as a guest artiste with local choirs and has also shared the stage in variety shows with Ivor Emmanuel, Rowland Jones, Stuart Burrows, Stan Stennett and Owen Money, to name but a few of the celebrities that have performed at The Grand Pavilion. Evelyn sang the well-loved Vera Lyn songs of the war years in the 1994 *We'll Meet Again* concert, as well as representing and entertaining the Townswomen's Guild at their Federation concert in 1992.

Left and below left: Professional artistes that have performed in The Grand Pavilion. Husband and wife team Patricia O'Neill (soprano, *left*) and Patrick Wheatley (baritone, *below left*). At twenty-one years of age, Patricia had the distinction of not only winning the soprano competition at the twenty-fourth Miners' Eisteddfod, but also of becoming the youngest ever champion soloist.

Below right: Nigel Hopkins is in his dressing room at The Grand Pavilion during the performance of *La Bohème* in 1992, has been involved in the world of grand opera for many years. He has travelled extensively with his concert tours in this country, Europe and the American continent. Quite recently, Nigel, with his daughter Nina as accompanist, has released a CD of his favourite songs and arias.

More local talent treading the boards of The Grand Pavilion.

Right: Representing the Townwomen's Guild as 'The Andrew Sisters' in the 1994 *We'll Meet Again* concert. From left to right: Leona Davies, Linda Peate and Gaynor Joseph.

Below: Barbara Powell née Seddon (left) and Marilyn Richards (right) in the 1959 production of *Magyar Melody*.

Below right: From left to right: Gill Frost, Norma Rees née Roberts and Carol Head née Ash in *White Horse Inn* 1961.

The talented Angell family of Kenfig Hill.
Sisters, Yvette and Nicola (*above left and right*
respectively) and parents Pat and Wyndham
(*left*). For many years the whole family was
involved with RAFA club and Porthcawl
Amateur Operatic and Dramatic Society
productions in The Grand Pavilion. As well as
taking active parts in these productions, Pat was
the seamstress for eighteen years.

Above: 'Put me in the back room where the girls are!' The Chorus of the Porthcawl Amateur Operatic and Dramatic Society's production of *My Fair Lady*, 28 April 2003.

Right: Two of the stars of *My Fair Lady*, Sue Bond (Mrs Pearce) and Heather Protheroe (Eliza Doolittle), 28 April 2003. Heather is also involved with scenery design.

Left: Nigel Lewis-Davidson, the 'Stanley Holloway' of Porthcawl. As Alfred P. Doolittle in *My Fair Lady*, he gave a fine rendering of 'I'm getting married in the morning'. It would have made any cockney envious!

Below left: Sue Bond is waiting for her cue in the wings, getting ready for her role as the wicked orphanage governess, Mrs Hannigan, in *Annie*, 8 October 2003.

Below right: This couple are performing in a skit from a 1970s RAFA show; Brian Davies as a Boy Scout, is miming to the song 'I believe' with Elaine Thissen. Brian was a stalwart of the RAFA club shows for over eighteen years.

Many famous stars have also performed at The Grand Pavilion. These have included Cilla Black (*above left*), Janet Brown (*above right*), and Ken Dodd (*right*).

Above: The Beverley
Sisters performed at
The Grand Pavilion
in 1991.

Left: Ruth Madoc of
'Hello Campers!' fame
has also entertained here.

Other regular visitors to the venue have included Joe Pasquale (standing) and Wayne Dobson, seen here with Jan Adkins, the General Manager, 10 May 2003.

Another well-known Welsh artiste and performer is Shân Cothi. She is seen outside
The Grand Pavilion prior to her appearance as a special guest on the *Peter Karrie and Friends*
production, during its countrywide tour of 2003.

A very entertaining act at The Grand Pavilion on 12 September 1999, was Paul Daniel's *Magic Show*. An artiste with a very warm personality, Paul is seen here cracking a joke with Mrs Malvina Morgan, while autographing his photograph for her.

Paul Daniels' other half in the husband and wife team making up the now famous *Magic Show* is Debbie McGee. Debbie first performed at The Grand Pavilion as a dancer in Stan Stennett's summer show of 1973. As a 'box jumper', a magician's assistant who jumps out of various boxes during the magician's act, she appeared on Paul's show and eventually married him. Like Paul, Debbie has a very pleasant personality and mixes easily with her fans.

Danny La Rue (*right*) is a regular and well-known visitor to The Grand Pavilion, and needs no introduction. The Grand Pavilion also seems to be a magnet for artistes from down under, with stars from the Australian soaps following in each other's footsteps to perform in the Christmas pantomimes. Ian Smith of *Neighbours* (*below left*) made the trip in December 1999 to take part in *Jack and the Beanstalk*, while Richard Grieve (*below right*) also of *Neighbours* and *Home and Away*, travelled here for the 2003/04 production of *Beauty and the Beast*.

Three more famous Welsh stars who have graced the stage at The Grand Pavilion.

Left: Siân Phillips, well-know for her starring roles in *I Claudius* and *Marlene*, appeared as recently as June 2003 in a solo performance entitled *Falling in Love Again*.

Below left: Mike Doyle cut his teeth at The Pavilion and has had a strong affection for the venue ever since.

Below right: Another well-known performer who needs no introduction is Wyn Calvin.

Right: The *Peter Karrie and Friends* show is a regular at The Grand Pavilion. Before each show Peter runs a talent contest among local artistes in order to select one to include in his evening performance. For the September 2003 show, Angharad Lewis was chosen to take part. Angharad is a mathematics teacher from Clydach, and is shown with Peter (centre), and Jeff Guppy, musical director.

Below: At the start of the 1970s, Stan Stennett ran the first of his summer shows at The Grand Pavilion. He is seen below 'performing' with Stan's People Dancers in the 1970 *Summer Stars* show. Many of the dancers in the group were local young ladies.

Above: In his show *Peter Karrie and Friends*, Peter encourages young local talent to take part in the production. For the 2003 performance at The Grand Pavilion the junior section of the Bridgend Youth Theatre, 9-14 years, were invited to take part. They are shown here practicing before the performance in the Jubilee Rooms, with Mrs Mary Jeffrys, Director, and Mr Paul Greenway, musical director.

Left: The Porthcawl Amateur Operatic and Dramatic Society also encourages young talent in its shows. Their production of *Annie* was a fine example of this policy, and many children took part in the orphanage and other scenes. Because of the current work laws protecting child actors, the part of Annie, the little orphan, was played to perfection on different nights by two young ladies. One of these, thirteen-year-old Jessie Scott, is shown here with another example of local talent, Sandy the dog, played by Bobby. A golden retriever owned by Amanda Hemsley, Bobby, was also a perfect example of how an extra should behave on stage, and he was allowed to take part in all of the performances!

Above: The management of The Grand Pavilion has the encouragement of young talent high on its agenda and operates a number of schemes to promote interest in the theatrical profession at an early age. With this in mind, a theatre workshop with the Bridgend Youth Theatre was initiated in February 2004. The workshop accepts children aged from seven to thirteen years from the Bridgend catchment area. This picture, by Malcolm F. Nugent, captured such a group of children with their class tutors, Raul Arrieta (staff member of The Grand Pavilion), and Xenia Christoforou.

Right: An example of young talent on the way up is Lauren Adams of Bridgend. Lauren, shown here in her role as Beauty in the Christmas 2003 pantomime *Beauty and the Beast* at The Grand Pavilion, began her stage career at the age of five when she started dancing lessons. She was only seventeen when she discovered her talent for singing and gave her first performance at St David's Hall, Cardiff. Lauren made her first professional appearance when she was nineteen, as a soloist with the Cardiff Philharmonic Orchestra. Since that time she has appeared in a previous panto' at The Pavilion and has toured with various productions as well as appearing in many television programmes.

There are many organisations in the local area that encourage youngsters to take up a life on the stage. Foremost amongst these is the Gloria Hill Academy of Dance, based in Bridgend. Run by Gloria Hill herself, she accepts both junior and senior pupils and has been providing dance groups for the pantomimes and other shows at The Grand Pavilion for the last ten years.

Left: From *Show Time 2003,* this shows Gloria Hill with a reluctant fairy. Maybe one day this little fairy will be able to cast a magic spell and turn herself into another Catherine Zeta-Jones.

Below: Another scene from *Show Time 2003* entitled *Hi Calamity*.

Above: The 'Jones' page; two famous examples of homespun Welsh talent that have reached the very top. Catherine Zeta-Jones first came to public attention in her role as Mariette in the TV production of *The Darling Buds of May*. She started her acting career when she was twelve years of age. The talented teen' had taken part in a pantomime at Swansea and trod the boards as a dancer in The Grand Pavilion around the same time. What a shinning example for today's young dancers. She is captured here, after her debut in the West End, by photographer John Fry in 1992.

Right: Tom Jones' experience at The Grand Pavilion in November 1963 must have made a great impression on him as soon afterwards he changed his name. On that evening Billy J. Kramer, the pop idol of the day, had taken centre stage to a packed auditorium of screaming teenage fans, made up mainly of girls, one would assume. The supporting act, a young vocalist and his backing group the Senators, did not have the same impact on the audience and the vocalist received no response from the horde of Kramer fans. Billy J. Kramer is now a memory to most of us, but the young vocalist, Tommy Scott, went on to thrill the world with his singing, as, who else, but Tom Jones! Anthony L. Tobin of Litchard provided this gem of information, and the current photograph of a new revitalised Tom is by Rankin and supplied by Valley Music Ltd.

Above: Wales abounds with talent. Vocal artiste Iris Williams has performed at The Grand Pavilion on a number of occasions. The most recent was in September 2003, when she gave a concert with the Porthcawl Male Choir. Made an OBE in the Queen's New Year Honours 2004, Iris has achieved worldwide fame with her singing. A scholarship to the Royal Welsh College of Music and Drama helped to launch a career that has included performances and TV appearances in over nineteen countries. Iris especially warms to a Welsh audience, whether at home in Wales, abroad or on board one of the many cruise ships on which she currently entertains.

Left: Last but not least, 'I was there!' Max Boyce. Yes, he was there, or rather here at The Grand Pavilion. A regular performer at the venue, his last appearance in 2002 was, like Iris Williams, as a guest of the Porthcawl Male Choir. Max is yet another one of Wales' great all-round entertainers. Known throughout the world for his rugby prowess, albeit in song and not on the pitch, Max ranks with the greats as one of Wales' famous and best-known emissaries.

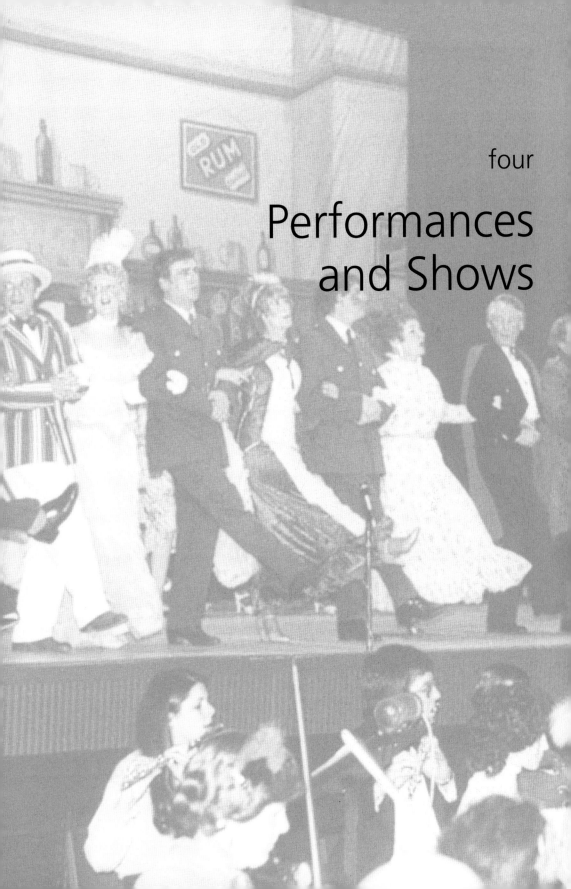

four

Performances
and Shows

The Grand Pavilion was designed to be a venue for relaxation, entertainment and enjoyment. The concert hall under the octagonal dome initially had seating for 1,350 persons, as well as a sprung floor for dances. To most people who remember The Grand Pavilion in the early days, it is the dances that come to mind first. Typical of the early dance bands that performed there is Harry Danell, with E. Hughes Davies on the organ and Bill Watts on trumpet. The two posters speak for themselves.

During the Second World War, as a young girl, Doreen Owen of Porthcawl regularly attended the dances held each week in The Grand Pavilion. She recalls that they were every Monday, Wednesday and Saturday. Dance nights would start with the playing of the organ prior to the house band coming on. The band at the time was the Jack Morgan Band (*above*) with Jack (*below left*) on double bass and his wife (*below right*), a great mover, who had a tendency to jump up and down while playing the piano.

Ellen Murphy (*above*) was the vocalist with the Jack Morgan Band, while Evan John and Dave Williams (*below left*) provided the musical accompaniment. A favourite with the patrons was the playing of the La Fleur Theatre Organ by Glan Evans (*below right*).

The Grand Pavilion has been a great place for romance. Many couples eventually married as a result of meeting each other on the dance floor there.

Above left: Ceinwen and David John Thomas met when David was stationed at RAF Stormy Down in 1941. They married in 1943 and now live in Penprysg, where they celebrated their diamond wedding in 2003.

Above right: Doreen and Benjamin Owen of Porthcawl are of a later generation; they met in 1949 at a dance in 'The Pav' as it was called, and subsequently tied the knot.

Left: Another couple who owe fifty years of happy marriage to The Grand Pavilion dances are Audrey and John David of Newton. They are shown in 1974 when John was chairman of Porthcawl Urban District Council and Audrey was his Consort.

The Grand Pavilion is still home to dancing, and both local and visiting bands perform here at regular intervals.

Above: Doreen Owen with members of the String of Pearls orchestra in September 1993.

Below: The New Squadronaires were captured on film by the author when they played at The Pavilion on 9 August 2003. A local band that performs at many weddings and other functions held in The Grand Pavilion is the Phil Dando Band (not shown). This band was chosen to play at The Grand Pavilion's Seventieth Anniversary Celebrations in 2002.

Where are they now? Do you recognise any of the actresses that took part in *It's Crazy*, one of the early shows performed at The Grand Pavilion? The presentation, which was by the Porthcawl Youth Club, took place on 24 July 1941, almost halfway through the Second World War. The picture includes many young actresses that went on to perform as adults in other amateur productions, after the end of hostilities. Seated centre with Howard Saunders on her right and Peter Oliver on her left, Sheila Gammon née Phillips, later initiated the *Porthcawl Steps Out* shows. The Porthcawl Youth Club was located in Lifeboat Road and was open six nights a week to boys and girls aged 11-20 years.

A group of charming young ladies who performed 'The Gold Fish Dance' in the underwater ballet scene of Sheila Gammon's née Phillips 1952 production of *Porthcawl Steps Out* photographed in the Winter Gardens of The Grand Pavilion. Do you recognise any of them? When Sheila put on her first *Porthcawl Steps Out* show in August 1946, the local press praised the school talent that shone in the performance and quoted Sheila as Porthcawl's youngest producer. Such shows were to provide both enjoyment for all and opportunities for young talent in Porthcawl for many years to come.

The cast of the *Porthcawl Steps Out* show at The Grand Pavilion in 1956. The photograph contains a galaxy of talent with many youngsters in the foreground. Do you recognise yourself or any of your friends in this show?

Left: Many of the performers that took part in the successful *Porthcawl Steps Out* shows also took part in the equally successful RAFA club shows. This was during the 1968 RAFA show at The Grand Pavilion. Norma Rees née Roberts is on the right with an unknown performer.

Below: Many local stars can be recognised in this photograph of the 1969 RAFA show, *Invest It 'ere,* at The Grand Pavilion.

Above: 'Les Girls' of the 1969 RAFA show at The Grand Pavilion.

Below: Performers from the 1968 production demonstrating their skills.

The cast of a RAFA show held at The Grand Pavilion in the late 1950s, during Battle of Britain Week. The show was produced by Howard Saunders, who is shown holding the bouquet just in front of the actor playing 'Justice'.

Above: Another RAFA show at The Grand Pavilion, but how good is your memory? What show is it and in what year was it performed?

Right: Members of the cast of the 1980 RAFA show during rehearsals, enjoying a break in the sunshine outside The Grand Pavilion.

This line-up of glamorous Chorus girls shows that no expense was spared in order to put on the best show. For all their presentations at The Grand Pavilion by the RAFA club, costumes were hired from professional theatrical suppliers in London.

A typical comedy skit from the RAFA show version of *South Pacific* at The Grand Pavilion. From left to right: Brian Webb (Steel Company of Wales), Tudor Sparks (of Sparks Motors, Mary Street), Brian Davies (of Barber Shop fame, Mary Street), and Glyn Thomas (one time manager of Trecco Bay Caravan Park).

The cast on the opening night of the RAFA club's *Flying High* show at The Grand Pavilion, 1954.

In 1982 the Gala Entertainment at the Palace of Varieties (alias The Grand Pavilion) helped to provide a substantial boost to the Mayor of Ogwr's Laser Beam appeal.

Above: The cast dressed in their old Musical Hall style costumes, assembled in the Victoria Rooms before the start of the performance.
Below: This picture captures the cast in full swing during the show's finale.

The Gala can-can girls! The Chorus line of the 'Combinations' dance troupe are, from left to right: Raye Greenway, Janet Lewis, Janet Aldridge, Yvette Angell, Gill Gore, Karen Addicott, and Sylvia Smith.

'Dancers save the show' was the caption that accompanied the photograph in the 18 February 1982 issue of the *Glamorgan Gazette*. Heavy snow almost prevented the Gala Entertainment taking place. If not for the determination of the girls, this probably would have happened. However, they had guaranteed 'it will be alright on the night' and made sure of this by walking up to seven miles in the snow to attend rehearsals. Peter Hubbard-Miles, the Master of Ceremonies for the Gala show, is here with Yvette Angell of Kenfig Hill (left) and Sylvia Smith of Porthcawl. The Palace of Varieties show was expected to raise more than £500 for the Mayor of Ogwr's Laser Beam Appeal.

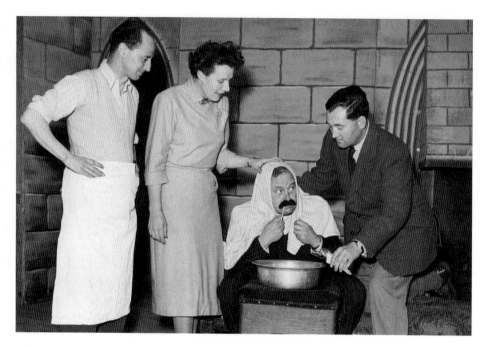

Above: Another organisation that favoured The Grand Pavilion with its presentations was the Porthcawl Little Theatre. This group was formed in 1948 and held its Inaugural Dinner at Comley's Restaurant on 12 May of that year. The very first of the Porthcawl Little Theatre's presentations, *Night Must Fall,* a play by Emlyn Williams, was performed at The Grand Pavilion on Friday 17 September 1948. They were a very prolific group and many more plays followed in quick succession, including *The Shop at Sly Corner, The Barber and the Cow, The Virgil, Dear Octopus,* to name but a few. The photograph captures a scene from the Porthcawl Little Theatre's production of *Castle in the Air.*

Right: Moira Anderson, the famous Scottish singer, performing on stage at The Grand Pavilion, 20 May 1979.

Below: The Richard Williams Choristers also appeared with Moira Anderson in the same show.

Opposite below: The South Wales Opera Company brought grand opera to the stage of The Grand Pavilion in March 1992. Puccini's opera, *La Bohème*, was presented there on four nights. The well-known soprano, Patricia O'Neill, took the lead role of Mimi under the musical direction of Clive John, who also conducted the orchestra. The presentation was produced by Patrick Wheatley. From left to right, seated: Brendon Wheatley, Patricia O'Neill, -?-, Nigel Hopkins and Patrick Wheatley. The Chorus was made up of local people. The Directors of the South Wales Opera Company were husband and wife team, Patricia O'Neill and Patrick Wheatley.

The Beverley Sisters, captured in full harmony by the author during their stage presentation at The Grand Pavilion in September 1991.

Many popular groups have performed at The Grand Pavilion, including The New Christy Minstrels, shown here during their performance on Friday 28 September 1979.

The Grand Pavilion has been the venue for many choral concerts. This photograph shows the Bridgend Police Choir accompanied by the British Steel Corporation Band at a concert they gave in November 1978.

The South Wales Burma Star Choir at a concert they gave at The Grand Pavilion on 14 October 1952, before going on tour to Canada and the USA. The guest artistes sitting in the centre were Evelyn White, Porthcawl, (soprano), and on her left Hayden Mizen, Pentrhydyfon, (baritone). The Male Choir was supported by the Bridgend (now Penybont) Ladies Choir.

Welsh diva, Iris Williams, being welcomed to The Grand Pavilion by members of the Porthcawl Male Choir Ladies Section Committee, prior to her concert there on 20 September 2003. From left to right: Mrs Meryl Evans, Mrs Olive Walters, Iris Williams, two of Iris' friends, and Mary Ellen Devery, Iris's agent.

Iris Williams in full swing on stage at The Grand Pavilion, backed by the Porthcawl Male Choir. Well deserved of the OBE that she was awarded in the 2004 Queen's New Year's Honours, Iris is a great performer and warms to an enthusiastic Welsh audience.

The Mayor of Porthcawl, Cllr Miss K. Rosemary T. Deere, congratulating Welsh diva, Iris Williams, after her fabulous performance at The Grand Pavilion on 20 September 2003. Iris had been invited to give a concert in The Grand Pavilion by the Porthcawl Male Choir.

Iris Williams with her musical director and Accompanist Peter Day (fourth from left), and the Peter Day Quartet. Iris is another star performer that encourages young talent. For this occasion she introduced Tim Murray on Trumpet (far right) who performed with the quartet and as a soloist. Like his promoter Iris, Tim is a product of the Welsh College of Music and Drama at Cardiff.

The Porthcawl Male Choir performing their first concert at The Grand Pavilion in November 1980.

Above: The Porthcawl Male Choir – Côr Meibion Porthcawl – on stage for their presentation of 'Iris Williams in concert' at The Grand Pavilion in September 2003. The president of the choir is Glan Davies and the chairman, Owain Jones. The choir musical director is Mair Jones and choir accompanist, Elizabeth Thomas. The compère for the concert was David Newton-Williams.

Opposite: In 1970, Stan Stennett brought South Wales' first ever summer show to The Grand Pavilion when he presented *Summer Stars* with a galaxy of stars and local talent.

GRAND PAVILION

MAIN PROMENADE — PORTHCAWL — TEL. 3860

PORTHCAWL'S CENTRE OF ENTERTAINMENT

FOR THE SUMMER SEASON, COMMENCING TUESDAY, 30TH JUNE, 1970
S.S. PRODUCTIONS PRESENT

SOUTH WALES' FIRST SUMMER SHOW

STAN STENNETT

COMEDY STAR FROM
THE BLACK AND WHITE MINSTREL SHOW

IN A SPECTACULAR PRODUCTION

Summer Stars

WITH JOHNNY TUDOR THE NEW RECORDING STAR

THE FALCONS

PAULA LEE AND ROY LESTER

LESLIE KING

JUDY FIELDER

★ THE MINSTREL SPOT ★

★ The BALLET MONTPARNASSE ★

The FABULOUS DANCING WATERS

CURRIES FAMOUS SPECTACLE

PRODUCED BY STAN STENNETT.   Full details and booking form overleaf. ➡

Stan's Gang rehearsing on the roof terrace of The Grand Pavilion for the first performance of *Summer Stars*, 1970.

From left to right: Johnny Tudor, Lesley King and Stan Stennett performing with the Ballet Montparnasse in *Summer Stars* at The Grand Pavilion, 1970.

Stan Stennett with guitar presenting his famous 'I'm a'riding' spot with Johnny Tudor and the Ballet Montparnasse in *Summer Stars* at The Grand Pavilion, 1970.

The full cast together with production and technical crews from the first of Stan Stennett's *Summer Stars* shows, 1970.

A scene from the 1971 production of *Summer Stars* with Shag Connors and the Carrot Crunches performing on stage.

Stars and stage staff of Stan Stennett's 1971 production of *Summer Stars*. There are many familiar faces in the front row who still serve The Grand Pavilion enterprise.

Stan also produced pantomimes at The Grand Pavilion. The first of these was *Billy and Bonzo meet Robin Hood* in December 1970-January 1971. In the grand finale line-up, Stan Stennett as 'Billy' is standing in the centre, holding the first live 'Bonzo' with Bryn Williams, the well-known Welsh singer as 'Robin Hood', and Jennifer Shaw as 'Maid Marion' standing to his left. Roy Lester, who took the role of the Dame 'Aunty Maggie', is on Stan's right. As was the case with the *Summer Stars* shows, the pantomimes were a great success.

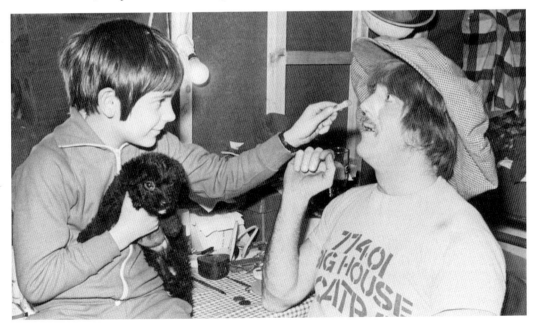

Stan Stennett 'Billy' and Ceri, his son, holding the very first 'Bonzo' in the pantomime *Billy and Bonzo meet Robin Hood*, 12 January 1971.

A scene from Stan Stennett's Christmas 1973 pantomime, *Jack and the Beanstalk*.

Stan as 'Billy', entertaining children from the audience on stage at The Grand Pavilion during the Christmas 1990 pantomime, *Dick Whittington*. The term 'pantomime' comes from the word 'pantomimus', which refers to a mime theatre in ancient Greece. The theatrical style as we know it today originated in Italy hundreds of years ago, from the Comiedia del'Arte. It gradually spread across Europe until it eventually reached our shores. Pantomimes are full of entertainment and give good value for money, as you have two performances for the price of one: that presented on the stage by the performers and that presented by the children making up the audience!

Above: The cast of the pantomime *Billy and Bonzo meet Babes in the Wood*, presented at The Grand Pavilion, 1991-1992. From left to right, back row: Johnny Dallas, who played the Dame, Jenny Ogwen and Lavina Smith. From left to right, front row: the Villain, the Babes, and Stan Stennett as 'Billy' with a stuffed 'Bonzo'.

Right: Stan Stennett taking centre stage in his usual role as 'Billy' during the pantomime *Robinson Crusoe* at The Grand Pavilion, 1992-1993. Always keen to promote young talent, Stan set up his own 'Stan's Gang' to give youngsters an early stage experience. For this pantomime, the Gang included a young Siân Rivers, who is shown seated on the immediate left of Stan.

Local dance schools were also encouraged to provide dancers to take part in the various shows and pantomimes held in The Grand Pavilion. The Dot Watts Dancers of Cardiff were regular performers with Stan Stennett and are shown here in tip-top condition during his presentation of the pantomime *Cinderella*.

Of a later generation, the Gloria Hill Academy of Dance, Bridgend, provides both junior and senior dancers for the current pantomimes and shows held at The Grand Theatre. The youngsters from this academy are very talented and the song and dance routines that they perform on stage are very professionally presented. The photograph captures junior dancers dressed for their 'Putting on My Top Hat' song and dance routine from *Showtime 2002*.

Christmas is the time for pantomimes. It is also the time for men to dress up as women and beasts, and for women to be transformed into Prince Charming. The 1994-1995 presentation of *Jack and the Beanstalk* at The Grand Pavilion was no exception to this age-old rule. In this production, Norman Robbins appeared as 'Dame Troy', Kevin Johns as 'Simple Simon', and Emma Booth as 'Princess Melody'. The cow chose to remain anonymous!

No pantomime would be worth its salt if it did not have a villain in the production. In *Robin Hood and the Babes in the Wood* at The Grand Pavilion 1995-1996, Stephen Lewis played the part of the evil Sheriff of Nottingham. Well known for his role in *On the Buses*, Stephen went on to play a character in the long-running TV series, *Last of the Summer Wine*.

Above: Pantomimes must also have a heroine. In a pantomime called *Snow White and the Seven Dwarfs*, who else but Snow White to steal our hearts! Maureen Nolan played this role in the 1996–1997 production by Paul Holman Associates. Her sister, Anne Nolan, took the part of the villainous (boo and hiss!) 'Queen Grizelda', the stepmother of Snow White. The ever-lovable seven dwarfs were very ably acted by members of the Gloria Hill Academy of Dance. The latter academy was also responsible for providing dancers for all the song and dance routines.

Below: Two scenes from the 1999–2000 pantomime, *Jack and the Beanstalk*. *Left:* Jo Castleton as 'Princess Marigold' with Ian Smith (Harold of *Neighbours* fame) as 'King'. *Right:* Roy Alvis as 'Dame Durden'.

Above: The part of playing the Dame is a very demanding role. Here we see Keith 'appy Hopkins in his dressing room making-up for his part as 'Dame Kitty' in the 2003-2004 pantomime at The Grand Pavilion, *Beauty and the Beast*. Once the make-up had been applied, it had to remain in-situ and intact throughout the performance. In addition to playing 'Madame Kitty', Keith was also director of the show.

Below: Not only must Keith's make-up stay intact, it must also allow for a change of costume. The Dame's costumes are always very elaborate and Keith undertook at least ten changes of costume during the performance – no mean task when he had to race up and down the stairs backstage to reach his dressing room in order to change in time for his next appearance, and the appearances were often in very quick succession. For this reason, Keith was the only one in the show to have his own personal wardrobe supervisor, Louise Viney, who incidentally, also spent a lot of time running up and down the stairs backstage to keep pace with Keith.

Left: Louise Viney is with Helen Jeckells as 'Witch Hazel' (left), choreographer Adrian Jeckells, associate producer, and Keith 'appy Hopkins attired in his finished Welsh-based costume for his role as 'Madame Kitty' in the first act.

Below left: Unless you have been on stage under the spotlights during a performance, you do not realise how hot it can get. Imagine having to dress up in a dog's costume and remain in it throughout the whole show. Well, that is what young Sadie Adams of the Gloria Hill Academy of Dance was required to do. She was not unmasked as 'Fluffy' the dog until the grand finale.

Below right: Andrew Piper also had to wear equally warm headgear for his role as the 'Beast'. He is shown with Lauren Adams who played 'Beauty' in the panto'.

Andrew is in his dressing room, preparing for the scenes that are to follow, in which 'Witch Hazel' turned him into the 'Beast'. The mask, in this case, was removable and did not require Andrew to make-up for the part. Nevertheless, with the claw gloves that he was also required to wear, Andrew found it very warm work performing on stage looking like nothing on earth!

The full cast of the 2003-2004 pantomime, *Beauty and the Beast,* together with production and stage crews at The Grand Pavilion, following completion of the final dress rehearsal the night before the show opened.

Many good productions have been presented at The Grand Pavilion by local organisations such as the Porthcawl Amateur Operatic and Dramatic Society (PAODS). Founded in 1924, except for a short period during the Second World War, the society has been giving regular annual shows ever since. The photograph shows the full cast of the Porthcawl Amateur Operatic and Dramatic Society's performance of *Magyar Melody* at The Grand Pavilion in April and May 1959. Where are they all now?

Since the 1930s, following the opening of The Grand Pavilion, PAODS productions have been presented at this venue. The 'Geisha' (*above left*) was put on there in 1960 and the photograph shows, from left to right: Joyce, Meryl, Norma and Jeff. In 1963 *The Three Musketeers* took to the stage with actors Ann, Carol, Norma and Ingrid (*above right*) taking part.

Oklahoma was presented for the first time in 1964 and featured local talent, from left to right: Betty Lewis (Ellen), Phillip George (Ike Skidmore), Molly Jones (Chorus), Emrys Davies (Chorus), -?-.

South Pacific is another production that has been presented more than once at The Grand Pavilion by PAODS. This scene is from the 1974 version and shows 'Captain Bracket' (centre), played by Lynn Davies, giving instructions to 'Lt Joseph Cable' and 'Com. William Harbinson', played respectively by Wyndham Angell (seated) and John M. Rees.

The cast of *Viva Mexico*, a very lavish production put on at The Grand Pavilion by PAODS in 1975.

The light operetta *Brigadoon* has been presented on two occasions at The Grand Pavilion. This is the 1976 show featuring Wyndham Angell (centre) as the star of the production, playing the part of the young American, 'Tommy Albright'.

The girls of the Chorus showing a leg in the 1980 Porthcawl Amateur Operatic and Dramatic Society's production of *The Pyjama Dance*.

The Porthcawl Amateur Operatic and Dramatic Society produced two shows at The Grand Pavilion in 2003: *My Fair Lady* and *Annie*. In the first of these, *My Fair Lady*, the role of the leading lady, 'Eliza Doolittle', was played to perfection by Heather Protheroe of Nottage. She is seen here on stage during Act I 'Outside Convent Garden', where her talent for clear English speaking with an exceptionally strong Cockney accent is detected by 'Professor Higgins' (Wyn Jones) on her right and 'Colonel Pickering' (Owen Harris) in full evening dress.

As Eliza's father in *My Fair Lady*, Nigel Lewis-Davidson gave a strong supporting performance and played the part of 'Alfred P. Doolittle' to a tee. His rendering of 'I'm getting married in the morning' would get him free drinks in any pub in London's East End!

Annie was another well-presented show by PAODS at The Grand Pavilion in 2003. To meet with the current work conditions that apply to young actors, the lead part of 'Annie' was played by two girls. In this scene, 'Annie' is joined on stage by Miss Hannigan, the governess of the orphanage, played by Sue Bond, and Victoria Roberts playing the role of 'Lily St Regis'.

The Hooverville and Parade children preparing to march from the foyer through the main auditorium, and onto the stage in Act I of the 2003 production of *Annie*.

The Porthcawl Amateur Operatic and Dramatic Society celebrated its eightieth anniversary with a presentation of Cole Porter's musical, *High Society*. The show ran in The Grand Pavilion from 27 April 2004 to 1 May 2004. It was way back in 1924 that PAODS was formed. The first show that it put on to celebrate its inauguration was the light operetta, *The Pirates of Penzance* by Gilbert and Sullivan. *High Society* was the ninety-second production – not bad going for a society that is made up entirely of amateurs! The photograph shows the leading lady, Victoria Roberts, as 'Tracy Samantha Lord' (the role made famous by Grace Kelly in the film version of the musical), surrounded by the girls of the household staff in Act I.

The eightieth anniversary team. The full cast of *High Society* with stage and production crews assembled after the show's full dress rehearsal on Monday 26 April 2004. The president of the Porthcawl Amateur Operatic and Dramatic Society is Dr David Parry. The chairman is Wyn Jones, who also took the part of Mike Connor, the reporter in *High Society*.

Porthcawl Comprehensive School is another prolific producer of shows that are presented at The Grand Pavilion. The management of The Pavilion participates with the Comprehensive School in an 'Industry and Education working together work experience programme'. Students interested in a theatrical career are encouraged to take up part-time employment in The Pavilion to learn the ropes of the trade. However, when it comes to show presentations, the school can compete with the best of them. *Gypsy,* presented at The Grand Pavilion in 1989, is an example of such a top quality show.

In 1994, Porthcawl Comprehensive School presented another spectacular show at The Grand Pavilion – *The King and I.*

The musical *Bye Bye Birdie* was the show that the Comprehensive School put on at The Grand Pavilion in 1993.

The presentation of *Fiddler on the Roof* at The Grand Pavilion in 1996 is a good example of the students designing and building their own stage set. The hand cart, incidentally, is a genuine antique. It originally came from Stanley Thomas & Sons, Plumbers, Porthcawl, and is always kept in The Grand Pavilion; see if you can spot it next time you visit the venue.

'The Trap family' and 'Maria', depicted by students of Porthcawl Comprehensive School in their presentation of *The Sound of Music* at The Grand Pavilion in 1999.

The ever-popular *Oklahoma* was another lavish presentation by the Comprehensive School in 2003. This photograph was taken during rehearsals for the show at The Grand Pavilion.

In February 2004, Porthcawl Comprehensive School tackled a classic hit musical story straight from the West End. Based on Victor Hugo's classic novel of the French Revolution, a new schools' version of *Les Misérables* had been released and this school was one of the first to take up the challenge. Performed entirely by students, over eighty took part and the very talented cast received a standing ovation at the end of the first performance. The production team was led by their director Romy Thomas, who was ably supported by musical director Linda Coombes, stage manager Hywel Owens and many others – too many to name – who all played a very important part. Over the years the school has produced many talented students who have gone on to carve professional theatrical or musical careers for themselves.

Porthcawl Comprehensive School has also given choral concerts at The Grand Pavilion and are shown performing at such a concert under the baton of their musical director, Linda Coombes.

The school also abounds with talent when it comes to the playing of musical instruments, and has a comprehensive orchestra made up of its own students. These students, together with professional musicians, provide the orchestral accompaniment to the many shows that the Porthcawl Comprehensive School puts on at The Grand Pavilion and other venues.

Not without imagination, the students of Porthcawl Comprehensive School (both male and female) have presented a very professional fashion show at The Grand Pavilion. All the fashions displayed on the catwalk were designed and modelled by the students themselves. What a wealth of young talent is being encouraged and promoted by the staff of Porthcawl Comprehensive School. With their academic, musical and artistic qualities, today's students are preparing to become the talented citizens of tomorrow.

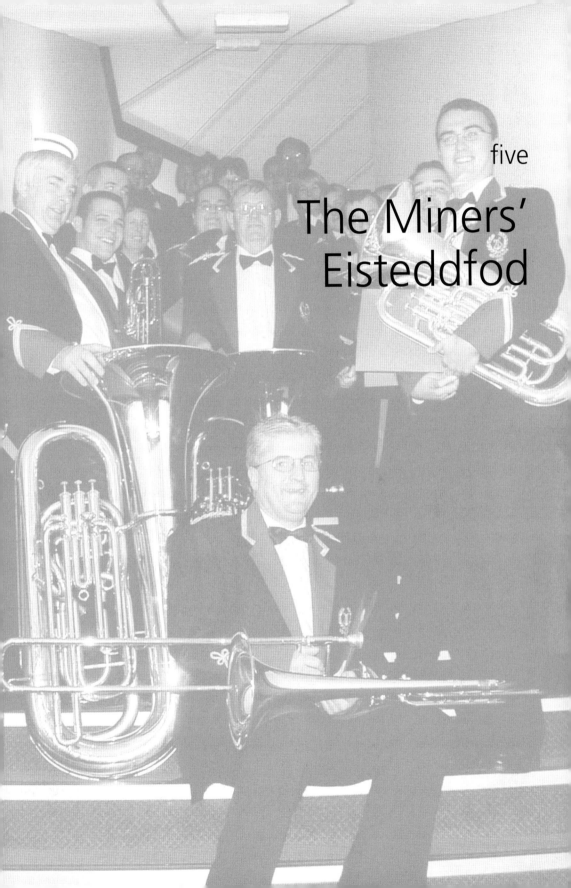

five

The Miners'
Eisteddfod

A capacity audience at The Grand Pavilion for a typical South Wales Miners' Eisteddfod. The original Eisteddfod commenced in 1948 under the auspices of the South Wales area of the National Union of Mineworkers. This was less than a year after the nationalisation of the coal industry, and was a tribute to the pioneer spirit of those behind the venture. The fiftieth anniversary of the Miners' Eisteddfod was celebrated in 1998 by introducing a Brass Bands Competition in order to bring a new musical dimension to the event.

Sadly, the once popular Miners' Eisteddfod has faded into obscurity and the Brass Bands Competition alone stands as a continuous living link with the original Eisteddfod. Organised under the patronage of the South Wales Miners' Eisteddfod, the Brass Bands Competition now takes place annually in The Grand Pavilion every February. It is supported by Porthcawl Town Council and Bridgend County Borough Councils, as well as the Coal Industry Welfare Organisation and Tower Colliery, Hirwaun.

Paul Robeson, 'honorary Welshman'. The links between Paul Robeson and South Wales were first forged in 1928 when he listened to a group of Rhondda miners who had marched to London to voice their plight. He promised them he would visit South Wales and did in 1939 when he made the classic film, *Proud Valley*. Persecuted in his own country under the McCarthy regime, Paul Robeson was unable to leave America when he was invited to take part in the 1957 Miners' Eisteddfod at The Grand Pavilion. Nevertheless, take part he did. A historic two-way transatlantic telephone link was set up direct from a studio in New York to The Grand Pavilion, from where he thrilled a capacity audience with his singing. In 1998, Dewi Roger Price, principal arts officer with the Brigend County Council, produced an audio tape of that momentous event. In this *Glamorgan Gazette* photograph by Howard Balston, Roger is holding the photograph of Paul Robeson which hangs in The Grand Pavilion.

Also in June 1998, Dewi Roger Price arranged for Paul Robeson Jr to visit Porthcawl. He was invited to officially open the 'Paul Robeson Room' in The Grand Pavilion. Paul Jr was very impressed with the memorabilia on display that commemorated his father's strong links with Wales. Of particular interest was the coal bust of his father which takes pride of place in this room.

Right: A young guitarist taking part in the 1978 South Wales Miners' Eisteddfod at The Grand Pavilion. The Eisteddfod catered for all musical aspects, both vocal and instrumental, and many a young artist's career was forged as a result of winning a competition at the annual event.

Below: The Porthcawl Male Choir competing in the choral section of the South Wales Miners' Eisteddfod in October 1982. The choir was first formed in 1980 and has been going strong ever since.

The Brass Bands Competition is now held every year in February. Bands enter from across Wales to compete for six cups. A secret draw is made prior to the commencement of the competition to decide the order in which bands play. The picture shows the draw selection being made in February 2004, under the supervision of the contest controller, Eifon W. Rogers (seated in the foreground). Unfortunately Eifon passed away shortly after the event, but his memory will always be associated with the Brass Bands Competition. Without his massive input, enthusiasm and commitment, it is unlikely that the event would have prospered.

The adjudicator for the February 2004 Brass Bands Competition, Mr Roy Sparkes (left), being led to his tent in the auditorium by senior competition officials, John Trottman (centre) and Cllr Mike Gray. Mr Sparkes does not know the draw order for the competing bands and is confined to his closed tent until the competition is over. It is at this time that he is allowed to emerge and present his findings on the qualities and ratings of the different bands.

Competition is fierce, especially as the quality of presentation by each of the competing bands is of the highest standard. This picture from the September 2003 event shows the pensive members of the Thomas Coaches Mid-Rhondda Brass Band relaxing on the stairs that lead from the Victoria Rooms to the stage, as they await their turn to compete.

The trophies are displayed on the stage dais throughout the competition and are: The CISWO (Coal Industry Welfare Organisation) Challenge Cup for the Winning Band; The Tower Colliery Cup for the Runners Up; The Doug John Cup for Third Place; The Eifion W. Rogers Cup for the Highest Placed First Section Band not included amongst the prizes; The Porthcawl Town Council Cup for the band with the most interesting stage presentation; and The Secretary's Rose Bowl for the best solo instrumentalist.

The secretary of the South Wales Miners' Eisteddfod, Mr Dewi Roger Price, welcoming the Mayor of Porthcawl, Cllr Miss Rosemary Deere, and the Mayor of the County Borough of Bridgend, Cllr Doug John, to the February 2004 Brass Bands Competition. Dewi Roger Price has been secretary to the South Wales Miners' Eisteddfod since 1974 and has been involved in this capacity with the Brass Bands Competition since its conception in 1998.

Tyrone O'Sullivan OBE, director of the Tower Colliery, presenting the Tower Colliery Cup to Richard Killen, the representative of the Tongwynlais Brass Band, February 2004. Tower Colliery, the last working deep pit in Wales, has been and still is a strong supporter and benefactor of the South Wales Miners' Eisteddfod and Brass Bands Competition. Tower Colliery, together with the Coal Industry Welfare Organisation, Porthcawl Town Council and Bridgend County Borough Council are all deserving of the thanks and credit that can be given to them for helping to maintain such institutions as the South Wales Miners' Eisteddfod and The Grand Pavilion.

six

Organisation and Services

This section of the book is devoted to taking the reader behind the scenes, so to speak, in order to show how The Grand Pavilion actually ticks! The staff of The Grand Pavilion, 30 September 2003. From left to right, front row: Jan Adkins – General Manager; Serena Williams – marketing officer; Julie Cane – general assistant; Pauline Hopkins – administration officer; Roger Price – retired principal officer arts and entertainment, Bridgend County Borough Council; Nigel Harding – duty officer. From left to right, centre row: Christopher Colquhoun – chef; Claire Harding – box office assistant; Michelle Hopkins – general assistant; Patricia Jones – general assistant; Lesley Burford – building surveyor, Bridgend County Borough Council. From left to right, back row: Wayne Francis – technical manager; Vivien Inglis – box office assistant; Martin Jenkins – retired General Manager of The Grand Pavilion; Andrew Lougher-Harris – stage manager; Anthony Callaghan – lighting technician.

The hub of the organisation is the general office, and it is from here that The Grand Pavilion is run. From left to right: Pauline Hopkins, Serena Williams, Jan Adkins, Wayne Francis.

The box office and reception desk is the first contact that patrons have with the staff when they enter The Grand Pavilion. The box office is manned by a team of staff throughout the week, even though there might not be any actual performance on at the time.

Above: Adrian Jeckells, associate producer of Paul Holman Associates Ltd (producers of the annual panto'), is chatting to Claire Harding and Vivien Inglis, box office assistants.

Below: From left to right: Claire Harding – box office assistant; Pauline Harding – administration officer; Georgia Thomas – general assistant/box office; three students on work experience.

No theatrical establishment would be complete without ushers and usherettes. The Grand Pavilion is no exception and this role is filled by general assistants. Julie Cane is in the centre with two students on work experience.

Every performance at The Grand Pavilion is fully supervised by a duty officer and team of general assistants. The roles are filled on a rota basis, on this occasion by Nigel Harding – duty officer, Patricia Jones (left) and Julie Cane (right) – general assistants.

General assistants have many tasks to perform during the presentation of a show. In this photograph one of the students has been captured doubling up as an ice cream seller during an interval.

Another example of job variation is the manning of the auditorium shop during a performance interval. A brisk trade in selling ice creams, sweets, and other treats is being carried out by the general assistant, Patricia Jones and a work experience student.

The Grand Pavilion also has a café facility, manned in the *top* photograph by Jacqueline Hopkins, and in the *above* picture by Michelle Hopkins and Katy Pask, who are all general assistants.

Right: The café provides a savoury and hot meal service, supported by an expert chef, Christopher Colquhoun.

Below: To complement its refreshment service, The Grand Pavilion has a fully licensed bar. Barman Peter Alexander is being assisted by Michelle Hopkins and Katy Pask while receiving encouragement from duty officer Craig Martin.

The real behind-the-scenes team: the technical crew. From left to right: Anthony Callaghan – lighting technician; Steve Dennis and Mark Phillips – technical assistants; Andrew Lougher-Harris – stage manager; Wayne Francis – technical manager. These are the lads that make the performances at The Grand Pavilion really come to life!

The engineering nerve centre of The Grand Pavilion: the lighting, sound and projection control room. This is situated at the rear of the balcony, from where an all-round view is obtained of the stage and auditorium. Wayne Francis technical manager (left) and Anthony Callaghan lighting technician, have complete control of the lighting, sound and all other technical facilities during a performance. The control box is also fully equipped with a film projector for occasions when The Grand Pavilion is used as a cinema.

Another technical facility which is not (understandably) obvious to audiences in The Grand Pavilion is the follow-spot room. This is situated above the control box, high inside the clock tower, and as demonstrated by Steve Dennis, can only be accessed with difficulty, via a vertical ladder.

The follow-spot room is equipped with two powerful spotlights which look down from their lofty position to follow and highlight the performers as they move about the stage. Hence, the derivation of the term 'follow-spot'. The two spotlights are being operated by Steve Dennis (left) and Raul Arrieta (right).

Organisation and management of all the stage activities are carried out from a control centre in the wings of the stage. Andrew Lougher-Harris (stage manager) is backstage in this photograph, setting up the control centre against the programme for Iris Williams' performance with the Porthcawl Male Choir on 20-21 September 2003. Nigel Newton-Williams, the compère for the concert, is in the background.

One of the many tasks carried out by the staff of The Grand Pavilion is the ongoing maintenance of the facility. The backstage area of the venue is not generally seen by the public, but has to be kept at a high standard for the benefit of the many artistes who visit and perform at The Pavilion. To these artistes, the presentation of their dressing rooms is of the utmost importance. In order to prepare and compose themselves for their performance, these rooms must be adequately equipped and have a very relaxing atmosphere. This requirement has been achieved by Craig Martin duty officer, who has decorated all the dressing rooms throughout, using very pale pastel colour schemes.

'Can I do you now, Sir?' For those of you old enough to remember Tommy Handley's Second World War *ITMA* stage and radio shows, Helena Colclough (left) and Breda (Brenda) Hole, are the 'Mrs Mops' of The Grand Pavilion. An invisible force to the general public that visit The Grand Pavilion, these two ladies provide a very necessary and important function – keeping the facility clean and tidy. The building must be kept spick and span at all times. It must be cleaned throughout before each show and, when there is more than one performance in a day, in between performances as well. They are two 'Mrs Mops' very worthy of Tommy Handley!

Always standing unobtrusively in the background of the auditorium at every performance held in The Grand Pavilion, members of the St John Ambulance Brigade provide an essential on-the-spot First Aid service for patrons. An organisation manned by volunteers, rank is no distinction when on duty, which can be seen in the photograph from the 1999-2000 Christmas pantomime, *Jack and the Beanstalk*. From left to right: Howell Harris – County Commissioner for Bridgend; Mrs Malvina Morgan; Ian Smith, 'Harold' of *Neighbours* fame; Mrs Violet Harris – auxiliary member.

Left: Raul Arrieta is teaching mime to children of the Bridgend Youth Theatre.
Right: A further facility encouraged at The Pavilion is the designation of selected performances which are interpreted by Clive Ellis in British sign language.

The Grand Pavilion team sorting out the initial photographs for the book. From left to right: Martin Jenkins (past General Manager); Keith E. Morgan (the author); Nigel Harding (duty officer); Jan Adkins (General Manager of The Grand Pavilion); Dewi Roger Price (retired principal arts officer, Brigend County Borough Council).

Cutting the celebration cake at the seventieth anniversary of the opening of The Grand Pavilion, August 2002. From left to right: Dewi Roger Price – principal arts officer, Bridgend County Borough Council; Cllr Doug John – Mayor of the County Borough of Bridgend; Jan Adkins – General Manager of The Grand Pavilion; Cllr Evan Williams – Mayor of Porthcawl. The anniversary Dinner and Dance was jointly organised by the local authority and the management of The Grand Pavilion. Music was provided by Phil Dando's Band and among the many celebrities and distinguished guests attending the function were Wyn Calvin and Stan Stennett, together with Patricia Mabley, the daughter of the late Cllr Russell Mabley JP, the founder of The Grand Pavilion.

Bewitched! One of the perks of being an author is that you get to meet such beautiful people! This was a spell-binding encounter with 'Witch Hazel' played by Helen Jeckells in the Christmas 2003 pantomime, *Beauty and the Beast*.

As a reader, I hope that you have also been bewitched by the contents of this book and have become enchanted with the aura of The Grand Pavilion. If I have achieved anything with this publication, it will have been to draw attention to the importance of this magnificent institution, not only to the people of Porthcawl and district, but to the thousands of visitors that have come to the town in the past and will continue to do so in the future. The Grand Pavilion is really Porthcawl's 'Jewel-in-the-Crown'. It is part of our heritage, and a gem that should be supported and maintained for generations to come.

Other local titles published by Tempus

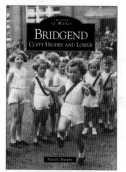

Bridgend: Coity Higher and Lower
NATALIE MURPHY

This collection of old images offers a unique glimpse into eras gone by, in the parishes of Coity Higher, Coity Lower and a small area of Newcastle Lower, from the turn of the century and over the subsequent 100 years. It is a chronicle of changing generations and shifting scenery, of outings, celebrations, Coronation parties or Wild West shows, and a reminder of the sacrifice of war, or the hardship of the 1960 flood.
0 7524 2653 2

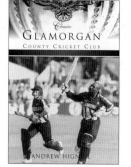

Glamorgan County Cricket Club Classics
ANDREW HIGNELL

This book traces the history of the club through fifty encounters that were particularly memorable, either for a great victory or a closely fought battle which ended in defeat. From Minor County matches at the end of the nineteenth century through to the triumphs of the year 2000, the games chosen can all be deemed 'classics'. Over 100 pictures have been chosen to illustrate these epic matches, showing key players, significant moments on the pitch and celebration.
0 7524 2182 4

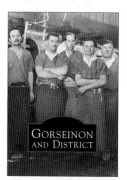

Gorseinon and District
KEITH E. MORGAN

This book charts the growth of Gorseinon and the surrounding district from a cluster of small agricultural hamlets into a thriving industrial community. It comprises over 200 archive images depicting all the different aspects of life in the area, from the pit winding gear and smoking chimneys of the local coal and steel industries to dance bands and day trips out in charabancs or half-cab coaches.
0 7524 2859 4

Swansea RFC 1873-1945
BLEDDYN HOPKINS

The 'All Whites' were founded in 1873 and became one of the eleven founder clubs of the Welsh Rugby Union in 1881. Swansea Rugby Club's history is renowned the world over for its many achievements. This volume traces the club's development from its formation through to the end of the Second World War. It gives a fascinating insight into the club and features team photographs, player portraits, action shots and many items of club memorabilia.
0 7524 2721 0

If you are interested in purchasing other books published by Tempus, or in case you have difficulty finding any Tempus books in your local bookshop, you can also place orders directly through our website
www.tempus-publishing.com